FOUR WOMEN.
FOUR JOURNEYS.
ONE POWERFUL COLLECTION.

OUR POWER
THE ANTHOLOGY!

KEBRA C. MOORE, VISIONARY

Attention: Permissions Coordinator

Welcome To The Storm Publishing!
info@midnightstorm.net

Ordering Information:

Quantity sales. Special discounts are available on quantity purchases by corporations, associations, and others. For details, contact the publisher at the email address above.

Orders by U.S. trade bookstores and wholesalers.

ISBN: 978-1-966612-53-7

Cover Design: Beenish Khan
Ambrose E, Ambrose E Editing Service
Author Headshot by: Sandra Brogdon

First Printed Edition: July 2025
Printed in the United States of America

Dedication

Dear TyKiah,

Thank you, my beloved soror, for courageously sharing your story with the world. I thoroughly enjoyed reading your journey and was deeply moved by your strength, transparency, and grace. I pray that your words travel far and wide while touching hearts, breaking barriers, and inspiring countless others to walk boldly in their truth.

You embody the true essence of our cherished sisterhood, Delta Sigma Theta Sorority, Inc. A woman of purpose, power, and profound resilience. Your contribution to this anthology is more than just a chapter; it's a testimony that will continue to uplift generations.

I look forward to witnessing all that's still to come! Because I know this is only the beginning. May your story continue to unfold in beautiful, powerful ways.

With love, pride, and sisterhood,

Kebra C. Moore
Visionary Author

Trigger Warning!

This anthology contains themes of sensitive topics.
Reader discretion is advised.

Contents

TyKiah Wright-Wilson

Former Commissioner for the White House initiative
on educational excellence for African Americans
Featured on the Montell Williams show
and winner of a national contest - Voices of Change
Publisher of DiversAbility Ohio - a coffee table publication
featuring leaders with disabilities
Founder & Chief Mentor - WrightChoice Mentoring Featured in Ebony Magazine as 30
Under 30

From where I sit

Introduction

From where I sit, the world has never been just one thing. It has been both beautiful and broken—expansive and restrictive, full of promise and full of barriers. I see it differently—because I live it differently. I move through life seated, but never stagnant. What others walk past without notice, I've had to navigate, question, and often fight to access. And while I was born into a world that wasn't built with me in mind, I've learned to reshape it—one bold choice at a time.

This book isn't just about living with a disability—it's about seeing the world through that lens. It's about what it means to constantly encounter inaccessibility, misconceptions, fear, and silence and to respond not with retreat, but with resolve. It's about the choices I've had to make, and the ones I've been proud to create for others—especially through the founding of WrightChoice.

From childhood through adulthood, my journey has been filled with contradictions: celebrated yet overlooked, resilient yet exhausted, visible yet unseen. I've learned to lead with my spirit, plan with purpose, and build bridges where doors were never installed. I've learned that sitting doesn't mean settling—and that mobility isn't only about moving your body, but about moving the world around you toward justice, inclusion, and equity.

In these pages, you'll read how I made sense of the biases I faced—how I wrestled with fear, met systemic inaccessibility face to face, and found my voice in spaces that often tried to quiet it. And how, ultimately, I turned those experiences into a vision—a vision called WrightChoice. Created not just to mentor young people, but to challenge the very structures that make mentorship essential for some and optional for others.

This is my story. But it's also a challenge, to look again at the world we move through. To ask whose perspectives are missing. To consider what might change if we saw each other not from above or below, but eye to eye. This is the view from here. From where I sit.

The View from the Classroom

I was born on June 3, 1977, in Columbus, Ohio. From the window of my childhood bedroom, the world always looked wide open—brimming with possibility, wonder, and adventure. That window didn't just frame the outside world; it shaped how I would come to see my place within it. Even as a small child, I sensed that my path would be different. And still, I never doubted that the world was mine to explore.

I was just a little girl when the world first began to treat me differently. My parents—overflowing with love, compassion, and hope—were heartbroken when, at just three years old, their only daughter was diagnosed with a rare condition called Charcot-Marie-

Tooth disease (CMT). This hereditary neurological disorder affects the peripheral nerves, weakening the muscles in the feet, legs, hands, and arms. At the time, we couldn't fully grasp how that diagnosis would shape not only the way I moved—but how others moved around me.

Before I turned three, life felt ordinary. I ran outside with my friends, made snow angels in the winter, and bounced around like any other child. But soon, red flags began to emerge. My parents noticed I was falling more than usual, and after countless doctor appointments—some local, others out of state—I was eventually diagnosed with peripheral neuropathy. Years later, we would learn the official name: Charcot-Marie-Tooth disease, a condition that affects roughly 1 in every 3,300 people and falls under the muscular dystrophy umbrella.

Although CMT is typically inherited, mine was one of the rare spontaneous mutations. My parents underwent genetic testing, and no family history of the disease was found. For years, I tried to make sense of it, even blaming my mom's smoking during pregnancy. While there's no definitive link between smoking and CMT, research does suggest it may contribute to certain genetic mutations or exacerbate related conditions. But in the end, there was no one to blame. It simply... was.

Since I was diagnosed at age three, I don't remember life without CMT. The news deeply shook my family. My parents had dreams and plans for me—and for a moment, it felt like all of that was interrupted by a future none of us had anticipated. But what they didn't know was that this diagnosis would become the catalyst for my strength and resilience.

Doctors weren't always kind or hopeful. One told my parents, *"Don't worry about teaching your daughter how to write. She'll be dependent on a typewriter for the rest of her life."* But my mother wasn't having it. Her response? *"What the hell does my daughter look like going through life not knowing the fundamental skill of writing?"* That fierce, colorful, and unapologetic stance became my anchor.

In fact, I became something of a medical anomaly. I remember attending muscular dystrophy clinics where doctors and medical students would gather around just to watch me write. To this day, it's still considered a phenomenon that I can hold a pen, given my lack of fine motor control.

My home was a split-level house, with stairs going both up and down. It wasn't accessible in the least, but the thought of moving never crossed my parents' minds. We made it work. I lived in that same home for 45 years. I learned the layout like a map—every carpet ridge, every smooth patch of linoleum, even the creaky floorboards and thresholds. The stairs were my Everest. I slid down them with a twist of my hips, pivoted at the landing like a gymnast sticking a dismount, and pulled myself into my wheelchair—my throne.

Our household operated like a well-oiled team. My brother was my first helper, doing my hair and helping me get dressed before school. My dad worked third shift, so he was home in the mornings to get me out the door and welcome me home after school with a snack ready. My mom, who worked first shift, returned in the evenings to cook dinner and hear all about my day. Our rhythm was precise, rooted in love and teamwork, and it stayed that way well into their retirement.

Because of my disability, I didn't move like other kids. I crawled, then I scooted, creating a rhythm of movement that worked for me. Bathing, grooming, and dressing all involved strategy. My father built a ledge next to the bathtub, making it possible for me to twist, pivot, and lower myself in and out. To use the toilet, I pulled myself up using my upper body strength. To brush my teeth, I knelt at the sink and balanced myself while brushing.

Despite my challenges, I insisted on doing my makeup myself. My hands lack dexterity due to the nerve damage from CMT, but applying my own makeup has always been my thing. It gives me pride, control, and confidence. There's something empowering about choosing how you show up in the world—especially when so much else is out of your control.

Hair, however, was a group project. From my mother and brother to friends, roommates, and personal care assistants, I've always had people who could follow directions well. Hair has always been a big part of my identity. People often recognize me as the girl in the wheelchair with the long hair. Back in the day, it was all about Pro-Con, Hot Six Oil, Pink Moisturizer, and swoop bangs into a ponytail. In college, when I was assigned a white personal care aide named Sarah, I panicked. "What am I going to do about my hair?" But God knew what I needed—Sarah was amazing. She followed every instruction perfectly and even introduced me to hair clips and new styles I came to love.

From kindergarten through fourth grade, I wore full-leg braces that stretched from the soles of my feet to the tops of my thighs. I wore them every day. They weren't just uncomfortable—they were heavy and brought constant stares and assumptions. Strangers often assumed I had cognitive delays because of the braces. It didn't matter that I was on the honor roll. One year, the school district required me to take an IQ test to determine whether I should be placed in a segregated school for children with disabilities. My family agreed, and I took the test—and passed with flying colors. That sealed the deal: I would be mainstreamed into general education, and no one would put me in a box again without a fight.

At most schools, I was the only student in a wheelchair. In middle school, I attended Eastmoor—a Columbus school with programming for students with disabilities. On the first day, a teacher's aide tried to take me to the orthopedically handicapped classroom. I told her, "That's not my class." She looked confused. When we got to the classroom, my name wasn't on the list. In classic fashion, I said, "Can I show you where my class is now?" I'd learned early on to speak up—sometimes with a little attitude when needed.

Eastmoor had two stories, but it also had an elevator, which meant I could fully participate in all my classes. That year marked my full transition to using a power chair. I got it in fifth grade, knowing I'd need it to navigate middle school with its multiple classrooms and crowded hallways. It took a while to get used to. At first, I parked the chair in the coatroom, walked around the classroom, and only used it to get home.

But eventually, I embraced it. My wheelchair became my equalizer—while others walked, I rolled. When they ran, I sped. I zipped through the hallways, kept up with my friends, and stayed cute while doing it.

Despite needing help getting dressed, groomed, and putting on my socks and shoes, once I made it down those stairs and did my signature pivot twist into my chair—I was off to the races. The chair didn't confine me; it freed me. It wasn't a limitation—it became a part of me. Not a burden, but a bridge.

The view from my childhood window taught me something essential: that home is where resilience begins. It's where dreams are born—not because life is easy, but because everything is possible. I learned to adapt. I learned to persevere. And I discovered that I could navigate the world—not in spite of my chair, but because of it.

This wasn't just a lesson I learned at home. It was a truth I lived every day—in classrooms, hallways, and cafeterias. My education wasn't only academic; it was deeply personal. I was learning to speak up, to be seen, to demand access, and most importantly, to belong.

The View from the Sidelines to the Stage

In high school, I dreamed of joining the cheerleading team. Growing up, I watched my older cousin cheer for Mifflin High School, and her enthusiasm inspired me to follow in her footsteps. By the summer after our sophomore year, my best friend Selena and I decided to try out for the team together. Tryouts were scheduled at the local recreation center, and in preparation, we created a cheer, practiced diligently, and perfected our routine to give the best performance possible.

The day of tryouts finally arrived, and we were eager to show the coaches what we had prepared. That week, I realized I needed wrist splints to support my arms and help me hit the motions with both strength and confidence. I can only imagine what the coaches were thinking as they watched a girl in a wheelchair give her all to a sport that traditionally had little to no representation of people like me. My family shared those same mixed feelings—my mom's response was a hesitant, "Oh… okay," full of uncertainty. Still, Selena and I moved forward with confidence.

When the results were announced, the coaches initially suggested that I could serve as the mascot. I respectfully declined, telling them, "I'm nobody's mascot." They withdrew the offer and instead placed me on the varsity team. It was new territory for all of us, but together, we adapted—and we grew.

This experience also sparked learning on a broader level, particularly within the school district's transportation department. I'll never forget our first football game. My family had to follow the activity bus all the way to Newark, Ohio. I told my parents, "This will be the first and last time you drive me to a game. No other parent is transporting their child—the rest of the team rides the bus."

By the next game, our athletic director and the transportation leaders developed a plan so I could ride the activity bus to and from all practices and games. This required a major adjustment—they weren't accustomed to assigning an entire bus route for just one student. The disruption was so significant that bus drivers began requesting the route, just to meet the girl who had inspired such a major shift in protocol.

Cheerleading began as a personal goal, but the outcome stretched far beyond what I ever imagined. I was featured on every local news station across the city. At first, I didn't welcome the attention. I felt like I was being "othered" for doing something others were doing too. It took time to understand the impact. Why was I being singled out just for choosing to cheer?

It wasn't until about a year after graduation that it finally clicked. I was at Northland Mall when a young girl in a wheelchair came up to me, excitement shining in her eyes.

"Oh my gosh! I saw you on the news when you were cheerleading! That's how I knew I could be a cheerleader too," she said.

She later joined her high school's cheer team.

Cheerleading competitions also had to adjust. At one event, the judges tried to disqualify our team because my wheelchair was used as the base of a mount. They claimed it was "too sturdy." But our coaches stood their ground. What started as me simply doing something I loved became a moment that challenged systems, redefined norms, and opened doors for others.

Throughout all four years of high school, I held one major goal: to walk across the stage at graduation. I've always had a deep desire to do things like everyone else. It might look different, but the outcome matters just as much to me. That desire became a muscle of perseverance—strengthened every time I took a bold step forward.

Senior year arrived faster than I expected, and it was time to put that perseverance into action. During graduation rehearsal, I began to form a plan. I enlisted three of my friends—Raeven, Yolanda, and Tanika—to help bring it to life. As vice president of the senior class, I'd already be on stage. And since my last name starts with W, I'd be the final student to cross. God couldn't have set the stage any better.

The moment arrived. The student before me had their name called. I nodded to Raeven and Yolanda. They knelt beside me, lifted me gently under my arms, and I took a step forward. The crowd erupted. Step by step by step by step, I made my way across that stage. I didn't even hear my name called—maybe it wasn't. When I looked up, Ms. Commodore was in tears. Mr. Johnson was speechless. No one had expected this.

I had told no one but my three friends what I planned to do. Tanika had one job: to roll my chair behind the curtain and around to the other side so it would be waiting for me. As soon as I sat back down, I whispered to myself, "Mission accomplished."

Gratitude filled my spirit. Another dream crossed off my list. For days, weeks, even years afterward, people would come up to me and say,

"You had my father crying at graduation."

Most recently, I was at a luncheon when someone asked if I had graduated from Mifflin High School. When I said yes, their face lit up.

"I remember when you walked across that stage."

One act of perseverance and self-determination created a lifelong ripple effect. But for every bold move, there was always someone nearby trying to clip the wings of my dreams. A counselor once told my parents, "Maybe your daughter should think about starting at a two-year college instead of a four-year one—because most people with disabilities don't finish four years."

From where I sit, that wasn't just a suggestion—it was a limiting belief disguised as advice. Once again, it was my parents who had to shut it down—with grace and strength.

By that point in my life, I was becoming more than just a witness to their advocacy—I was developing my own. I realized early on that the most powerful way to advocate for myself was through action.

I enrolled at Wright State University, where I spent six of the most defining years of my life. From the moment I rolled onto that campus, I was determined to lead, to leave a mark, and to make sure my presence mattered. Wright State was a special kind of place—one where students with disabilities weren't seen as outliers but as essential parts of the university's heartbeat.

Still, the transition from high school to college was daunting. I was leaving behind a support system that knew me inside and out. On move-in day, my family helped transform my dorm into a home. My childhood best friend became my roommate, which softened the blow of goodbye.

But there was no denying it: I was on my own now, and it was time for my life management skills to take center stage.

Thankfully, Wright State offered something rare—a Personal Care Assistance (PCA) program embedded in student life. Students were paid to support classmates with disabilities, making care more accessible and dignified.

My freshman dorm had a communal bathroom, which meant adjusting to shared routines and learning to lean into trust. From help with showers to haircare, I was discovering how to rely on others in a new way—without ever losing my sense of self.

Once I rolled out of my room and hit the pavement, I was flying solo and fast. Wright State even had an accessible on-campus bathroom staffed by PCA personnel, offering quick support throughout the day.

And my circle of roommates—who were also dear friends—stepped in like family. Whether it was Tselane wrapping my hair at night, Kendra sneaking over to adjust the thermostat on my behalf, or Celina cooking fried cabbage and sausage just like my momma, I never lacked love, laughter, or a hot meal.

From where I sit, college horror stories about unreliable aides or inaccessible dorms are all too common. But God's hand was on every part of my journey. Every attendant showed up. Every schedule was honored. Every need was met.

I zipped across campus like I owned it. Honestly? I kind of did. I mean—it was called Wright, after all.

There was nothing I wanted to do that I couldn't do. I joined the President's Ambassadors Club, worked in the Human Resources department, and even took bus trips—including a life-changing journey to the Million Woman March in 1997. I completed off-campus internships and squeezed every drop out of campus life.

My leadership blossomed during those years. I served on the Student Government Budget Board, allocating funds to campus organizations, and dared to dream even bigger. One of those dreams? Becoming a member of Delta Sigma Theta Sorority, Incorporated. In the spring of 1999, that dream came true.

It's rare to see someone with a visible disability pledge a Black sorority—but from where I sit, barriers are just invitations to build new pathways. Not only did I pledge, I rose quickly to serve as chapter president. I helped lead our chapter with pride, launching service initiatives and building a brand that reflected sisterhood, excellence, and visibility.

College also taught me how to show up in relationships. It taught me how to talk openly about my disability—not out of obligation, but from a place of power. Vulnerability wasn't weakness. It was trust. It was communication. It was courage.

And courage often showed up in hilarious ways—like the time Byrdie pushed me in my manual wheelchair down a hill in College Park. Well—not so much pushed. He let go and started running beside me, laughing as I picked up more speed than either of us expected. I flew down that hill, wild and free, the wind in my face—and just before disaster struck, he caught me. We laughed until our stomachs hurt. From where I sit, that moment was a metaphor: things might get out of control, but I'll always land safely—surrounded by people who truly see me.

One of those people was my mentor the late Jeff Vernooy. Jeff didn't just offer support—he offered strategy. He taught me what advocacy really looked like, not just for myself but for others. He showed me that my voice carried power, and that leadership isn't about standing tall—it's about standing firm in who you are, even from a seated position. Jeff helped me understand that access isn't a privilege—it's a right. And using my voice to demand it wasn't just brave—it was necessary.

If I shouted out every name that shaped my journey, this chapter would never end. But know this: they didn't just see the wheelchair. They saw me—my humor, my heart, my hustle, and my hopes.

Looking back, college wasn't just a chapter of education. It was a chapter of elevation.

From where I sit, it was the place where I found my voice, sharpened my leadership, and embraced my power—not in spite of my disability, but because of everything it taught me about showing up boldly in the world. I didn't just go to college. I owned my college experience.

The View from The Launch Pad:
Lessons, Letdowns, and a Leap of Faith

From where I sit, some of life's greatest breakthroughs don't come when everything goes right. They come from hitting walls—hard ones—again and again. And yet, you choose to rise. To try. To believe.

After graduating from Wright State University—a place where I found my rhythm, my voice, and my sense of leadership—I was eager to transition from student life to professional life. I was ready to launch a career in Human Resources, the field I had studied, trained in, and poured so much of my energy and time into. I had completed the internships, earned the degrees, and built the network. I had the receipts.

I was well-prepared—honestly, maybe even over-prepared. But I quickly discovered a harsh disconnect between being qualified and being chosen. The world I entered after college didn't reflect the equity I had experienced at Wright State. Outside the bubble of inclusion, I encountered something far more familiar to many disabled individuals: exclusion masked as politeness and rejection disguised as "concern."

Under-experienced. Over-educated.

Those were the labels companies used to soften the blow. They'd say things like, *"We're going in a different direction,"* or *"You're a great candidate, but..."*

But the truth was, I never fit the image of who they imagined in the role. Sometimes, I didn't even make it into the interview room.

There were job interviews where the interviewer had to come out and meet me in the parking lot—because the building wasn't accessible. No ramp. No elevator. Just stairs... and silence. Needless to say, there were no callbacks.

But from where I stand, rejection was never personal—it was structural. It was systemic. It reflected a workforce that was unprepared, unwilling, or uninterested in making space for professionals who moved through the world differently.

Still, I knew my worth. I knew what I brought to the table. And when the table had no room for me, I stopped trying to squeeze in.

I realized I needed to build a new table

This wasn't just about finding a job anymore. It had become about reimagining what a job could look like—about creating pathways for students like me: qualified, ambitious, and underestimated. I couldn't stop thinking about how isolating it felt to have the credentials but none of the access.

I thought back to high school and remembered applying to a summer internship program that was designed to connect underrepresented students with career opportunities. I had been so excited. My best friend and I submitted almost identical applications— we were both top students: articulate, driven, and eager. She got in. I didn't.

There was never an explanation, but deep down, I knew why. Even a program intended to uplift marginalized students hadn't been built with disabled students in mind. Not with someone like me. Not with physical needs. Not with a wheelchair.

It wasn't bitterness I felt—it was clarity. I tucked that experience away, knowing that one day I would build something different. Something inclusive from the very beginning. Something that wouldn't overlook students like me.

At the time, I thought that "someday" would come after I had climbed a few rungs of the corporate ladder, proven myself, and earned credibility. But God had other plans. The rejections weren't just setbacks; they were redirections.

One afternoon, sitting on my bed with my laptop open and my spirit heavy, I began jotting down ideas on a notepad. I wrote words like access, excellence, diversity, and internships. I didn't have startup capital. I didn't even know the legal steps to start an organization. But from where I sit, purpose speaks louder than fear.

With a blank Word document on my desktop and a fire in my belly, I drafted the very first mission statement for what would become WrightChoice. I didn't know I was starting a pivotal organization that would impact generations. I didn't have the words for it at the time. I just knew I was building what I had once needed—a door where none had existed.

I reached out to people I had met through internships, professors I had connected with, and mentors I had encountered during my college leadership roles. I asked questions. I took notes. I listened. I researched. I prayed.

And I learned how to build while flying.

And as I did, I became the person I had needed when I was sixteen, trying to land a summer internship. When I was twenty-two and striving to enter the workforce, I became a mentor, a connector, and a bridge.

WrightChoice wasn't born in a boardroom. It was born in my bedroom, out of frustration, faith, and fierce determination. It came from broken systems, missed opportunities, and deep personal letdowns. It was built from every "no" I ever received and every "yes" I never heard.

It was born the moment I stopped waiting to be included and started designing a world where I already belonged.

WrightChoice became a space where students, especially those with disabilities and from marginalized backgrounds, could access support, professional development, mentorship, and real career opportunities.

And the truth is, it started small: a couple of workshops, a few conversations, partnerships I had to earn, and meetings where I had to prove the need again and again. But I was used to that. I'd been proving myself my entire life. From where I sit, every setback in my life has carried seeds of redirection.

What once felt like locked doors now look like detours toward destiny. I didn't set out to become a founder or a changemaker, I just wanted a fair shot. When I didn't get one, I created one, for myself and for others. And just like that, what once felt like an obstacle course became my launchpad.

From where I sit, I found purpose.
From where I sit, I found peace.
From where I sit, I found love.
From where I sit, I found happiness.

But I never expected what—or who—would come next...

To be continued.

Final Message to Readers:
Hope, Resilience, and the Beauty of Owning Your Story

Your story however messy, painful, beautiful, or unfinished, it is worthy of being told. If CMT has taught me anything, it's that our storms don't cancel our purpose. In fact, they reveal it.

You may feel invisible at times. You may feel unheard. But you are here and that alone is a revolution.

Own your story, not just the triumphs, but the trials. That's where your power lives. That's where the truth is born.

To anyone walking, or wheeling, through the fog of uncertainty: keep going. Your pace is your power. Your difference is your gift.

There is beauty, even in the storm. And whatever you do, strive to make the right choices.

Acknowledgements

This book would not exist without the love, faith, and support of so many who have poured into my life, lifted me in moments of doubt, and reminded me that my voice—and my view—matters.

To God be the glory. Your grace has sustained me, your light has guided me, and your purpose has anchored every step of this journey.

To my husband, Edward Wilson, thank you for loving me fiercely and faithfully. Your partnership has brought a new level of joy and wholeness to my life. You remind me every day what it means to be truly seen and loved.

To my father Gary Sr., my heavenly angel, and my mother Pam—your unwavering support and sacrifices laid the foundation for everything I have become. You believed in my potential even when the world tried to place limits on it. You gave me agency to use my voice empowering me to advocate for myself and others with confidence.

To my brother Gary Jr., sister-in-love Terri and my beloved nieces Mikayla, Keeley, and Maya —thank you for covering me in prayer and reminding me of the power of family, love, and laughter. I carry you with me in every chapter of this story.

To my family, besties, girl tribe, sorors and friends —you have supported, celebrated, and pushed me forward. You've challenged me to grow and reminded me of the strength and love found in community. Your encouragement gave me the courage to write *From Where I Sit*.

To my WrightChoice family—past and present mentors, mentees, staff, volunteers, and partners—you are living proof that mentorship changes lives. Thank you for being part of this movement and for allowing me to walk alongside you as you discover your own strength and purpose. Thank you all for being part of my view.

With deep gratitude,
TyKiah Wright - Wilson

About the Author

TyKiah Wright-Wilson, MBA is a passionate social entrepreneur, speaker, connector, and advocate whose life and leadership have been shaped by her lived experience as an African-American woman with a disability.

As the founder of WrightChoice Mentoring, TyKiah has empowered thousands of young people to pursue their dreams through career pathway exploration, mentorship, and job placement. Her work centers on workforce development, access, and opportunity—helping youth and young adults envision and create a future filled with possibility.

TyKiah has held numerous leadership roles at both the national and local levels. She was appointed as a Commissioner to the White House Commission on Educational Excellence for African Americans under President Obama's Administration, served on the Board of Directors for Disability Rights Ohio, and was a member of the Board of Directors for the Wright State University Alumni Association. These roles reflect her unwavering commitment to educational equity, disability advocacy, and community empowerment. She is also a proud member of Delta Sigma Theta Sorority, Inc.

With a heart for leadership and service, TyKiah has built a legacy of inspiring individuals to see challenges not as barriers, but as building blocks. In *From Where I Sit*, TyKiah offers an unfiltered and powerful perspective on resilience, identity, and purpose—inviting readers to reflect on how they see the world, and how the world sees them.

TyKiah is the proud wife of Edward Wilson, and a devoted daughter, sister, aunt, cousin, niece, and friend. She is a woman of deep faith and a relentless believer in what is possible—from any seat at the table.

How to Connect with TyKiah:

LinkedIn: TyKiah Wright- Wilson
Facebook: @TyKiah Wright- Wilson
Instagram: @iamtykiahwright

Luticha Andre Doucette

Association of University Centers on Disability Emerging Leader
2020–2021 Rochester Institute of Technology Distinguished Alumni Awardee
Susan M. Daniels Disability Mentoring Hall of Fame Inductee

A Solitary Reverie

"Do You Know Where You're Coming From?"

At the time of this writing, I'm celebrating forty years of living with a spinal cord injury and traumatic brain injury. How does one compress four decades into just 5,200 words? How do I distill all the lessons and shenanigans into something meaningful? And how do I avoid centering trauma when so much of life has been shaped by it? But dear reader, let's take this journey together, perhaps we'll discover and reveal a few things along the way.

Maybe I could be dramatic and say: I was born, I lived, but clearly I ain't dead, because here I am writing this. As a Creole , understanding who I am often requires knowing where I came from. My aunt once told me this truth, and it stuck. Our past gives us the foundation for how we move through the world. The lessons we carry are not solely our own; they come from the generations before us. Their stories, flawed, messy--human--shape who we are.

I am a child of New Orleans and New Iberia, Louisiana. I am the second generation out of the Great Migration and the first generation out of Jim Crow. (Ironically, I'd argue we're now living in Jim Crow 3.0.) I was born into families that valued education, had no option but to work hard, and, above all, carried a fierce stubbornness, tenacity, and an insatiable curiosity that runs deep through our bloodline.

Like many with spinal cord injuries, I don't remember the day of my accident, though, clearly, I was there. It was Memorial Day weekend, 1985 (I was 22 months old), when life suddenly changed. For most of us, a spinal cord injury doesn't just upend our own lives; it transforms our families' lives, too. Yet the supports and services offered rarely reflect that reality. They're aimed solely at the individual, often ignoring the broader ripple effects of trauma.

I've never really seen a holistic approach to helping families navigate the chaos of acquiring a spinal cord injury, especially when that injury drops them into an inaccessible world and a healthcare system that barely qualifies as care.

And so, my young parents suddenly found themselves facing a new reality: their child in a coma, doctors bombarding them with dire predictions, telling them I needed surgery, telling them that even if I survived, I'd be nothing more than a vegetable. I once asked my mother if the doctors at least specified which type of vegetable. Her only reply: a swift, "Shut up, Luticha."

We were a military family, but it quickly became clear the military couldn't offer the kind of care I needed. So, transitioning to civilian life became necessary, for me to survive, and to receive the kind of support that might make surviving worth it.

California is where we landed, the land of sun and hipsters. After successfully advocating to get me off phenobarbital (which is now banned for use in children under age twelve), my parents moved to Yuba City–Marysville. This would become the place where many battles for access to education began and where my battles with my mother first took root.

But first, there was Shriners, in San Francisco. Supposedly world-renowned for their expertise with children with disabilities, it was the first place where I met kids my own age, and where my mother met other parents navigating similar struggles. I was admitted around the age of three or four, staying with my mom for about six months of rehabilitation. Rehab in the '80s was nothing like it is today. Back then, hospitals allowed longer stays so you could actually learn how to use a wheelchair and develop other essential life skills.

The staff thought aquatic therapy might be beneficial and tried to get me into the pool. But I was convinced that the black-and-white checkered bottom of the pool was made of pits of doom. I screamed that I was going to drown, that I'd sink into those bottomless pits. Clearly a sci-fi fan even then. I was eventually banned from aquatic therapy for disrupting the other patients. There was no real attention paid to why I was so afraid, only stern looks and sharp scolding from my mother, insisting these people were trying to help me.

It was at Shriners that I first began to feel hatred toward my body and detachment from it.

I remember it vividly: the first time they taught me how to catheterize myself. For those unfamiliar, catheterization is a technique where you insert a long, smooth plastic tube with rounded holes at the end, called a catheter, into the urethra to drain the bladder. They teach you how to do it yourself using a mirror.

Back then, they instilled the fear of God in us over two things: urinary tract infections and pressure ulcers. They had a book full of horrifying photos they used to drive the point home. It was like the hospital version of "This is your brain on drugs," but in this case, "This will happen to your body if you don't take care of it."

Even though they tried to make it more approachable, using an anatomically correct Cabbage Patch doll to help us understand our bodies, the pressure to get it right was overwhelming. There was no privacy, no time to process what was happening. You had to do it now, in front of a crowd, while a whirlwind of emotions stormed inside you.

My mother grew increasingly frustrated, telling me I needed to stop hesitating and just do what they said.

I cried even more.

My mom was upset and said that I had to practice and that this is life. "You sometimes have to do things you don't want to," she explained. She then took the doll and asked the folks to show her how to do it. After she was done, she asked me to try. I took the doll and the catheter and followed the steps. Everybody cheered. I became more sullen. I felt empty.

After we left Shriners, I refused to catheterize myself at home. This became a major point of contention between my mother and me. She was my primary caregiver, and I often bore the brunt of her frustration, anger, and exhaustion. As an adult, I can now recognize her humanity in all of this. Those early years of living with a spinal cord injury were filled with anxiety, fear, and deep frustration.

Still, it was hurtful, and it left irrevocable damage in our relationship. After one especially tense battle of wills over catheterization, she slumped in defeat and said, "I hate this." That was the closest I ever got to an apology. She never hit me again over it. She never forced me to cath again.

That moment stayed with me. Even now, I still struggle with the daily management of bowel and bladder issues, chronic pain, and fatigue. And sometimes, I find myself mumbling those same words: "I hate this." It's okay to feel frustrated about being disabled. Too often, toxic positivity invalidates those feelings, as if we're wrong for not loving ourselves unconditionally every day.

But let me be like Tina Turner and ask: what's love got to do with it? Last I checked, my bladder doesn't care whether I love myself, it just needs to function. We are human beings with needs, and those needs must be met, even if they fall outside the norm. That can be incredibly frustrating, especially during public accidents where there's no accessible bathroom to clean yourself in a way that restores your dignity.

Even at home, living alone, the weight of doing laundry and showering can be exhausting. I find myself mumbling those same words again and again. This is why we need community. This is why we need to advocate for quality caregiving. Not only should caregivers be paid a living wage, but with the current worker shortage, these everyday challenges become even harder. I can't tell you how many times I've heard stories of disabled people left sitting in their own feces or urine for hours because no caregiver was available to help.

We were trained for the convenience of the caregiver, not the natural rhythms of our bodies. During a worker shortage, those "training" protocols felt more like survival tactics. These experiences can lead to disassociation from your body and a deep, lingering self-loathing. Many people with spinal cord injuries experience higher rates of depression, not only due to social isolation but because the severing of the spine often coincides with the severing of family and community ties. Persistent inaccessibility drives that wedge even deeper.

That time in my life gave me a vision, a longing, for a world that truly cares about disabled people. A world where care needs are met. It also revealed how unequipped most people are to work with children, especially children with spinal cord injuries. At that time, we were far from the norm. Yet the expectation from hospital staff and my parents was that I should function within the same framework as the adults. That was unrealistic.

But enough pontificating.

Shriners had rules, like any hospital. But isn't that the way of disability in general? You're told what to do, when to do it, how to do it. Everything is rigid and regimented, from funding structures that dictate what you can or can't receive, to which levels of disability are considered "worthy" of support, to what you can use funding for, where you can go, and how you're allowed to be. And somehow, within all of that, they're supposed to be teaching you how to be independent.

Disabled life is always a contradiction in terms.

Lights-out happened at a set time. At some point, my mom and I stopped sharing a room because the staff believed she was hindering my progress. But soon, they ran into a problem: I wouldn't fall asleep. I'd sing to myself until midnight, becoming a disturbance.

My mother simply shrugged.

"I told you, if you let her watch Star Trek, she'll be asleep before the credits end. Not my problem if you won't listen to me."

So, they gave me a tiny TV to watch Star Trek and whatever else I wanted. Sure enough, I started falling asleep on my own.

There was a particular nurse I didn't like, according to my mom. She taught me how to use a wheelchair. When I refused to do it her way, she went to get my mom. My mother said she came in to find me repeatedly crashing into the wall.

The nurse was exasperated.

"Why do you keep doing this? That's not how you were taught!"

My mom laughed.

"She's doing it because she doesn't like you. I don't like you either. Luticha, go find your friends and stop bothering this woman. You won't have to deal with her again."

I beamed and, to the woman's shock, zipped away.

The kids and I formed a little gang, led by me. One time, we sneaked into the nurse's station. There we were, five kids in wheelchairs, crammed into a narrow space, oohing and aahing over the microwave and other forbidden treasures.

We got caught.

Tattled on by a girl we didn't like. As the nurse came to scold us, we tried to rush out, but we got stuck. Little kids in chairs were zipping away while this woman shouted like she was Trunchbull herself. I was the last one out, and as I passed by, the girl hit me. So, I pushed her back.

That push had consequences. I was forbidden from being around the other kids.

My mom explained it was because the girl had, i think cancer because I can't remember her diagnosis, and I could have seriously injured her. She reminded me that since I was stronger, I had to be extra mindful. Always.

I disagreed. I believed that regardless of your disability status, if you put your hands on me, you should expect an equal and opposite reaction.

But alas, I wasn't even five years old. I had to listen to my mother.

Instead, I spent time with her and some of the older patients, playing bingo and winning stuffies. On the days we saw other families, it was during craft night, where my mom outshone everyone with her boondoggle skills.

My mom also noticed something else, something that disturbed her deeply. My behavior wasn't the only reason I wasn't seeing my friends. Many had gone in for surgery, and afterward, they were on ventilators. The parent rumor mill suggested the kids were being used as teaching tools during surgery.

I have no idea if that was true. I also wouldn't put it past a teaching hospital at the time to do this.

Years later, I learned from nurse friends that in the '80s and '90s, disabled kids would sometimes crash or code in the operating room with no clear explanation. Many died. Others were saved by receiving a trach.

Eventually, they discovered the cause: unknown latex allergies. That's why there was such a massive push for hospitals to implement latex warnings.

My mother didn't know that at the time. What she did know was that she didn't want a repeat of what happened when I was first injured, doctors insisting on surgery and me waking up on a ventilator.

It terrified her. And she was determined never to let that happen again.

School Daze!

As I said, we come from a family that believes every member should be educated. Education was hard-fought, something denied to us, like it was to so many Black people and so the expectations for me, disabled or not, were no different than for anyone else in my family.

However, the school board disagreed. They recommended that I be institutionalized.

Now, this was before the Americans with Disabilities Act. While the Education for Handicapped Children Act, passed in 1975, was technically in effect, that didn't mean my educational needs were guaranteed respect. There's a vast difference between a law being passed and people actually valuing disabled people or any marginalized group, as human beings deserving of the same opportunities. There's a difference between having a right to education, and people wanting to educate you.

As a Black child, Brown v. Board of Education affirmed my right to classroom integration. Yet, in the late 1980s and early 1990s, institutionalization was still considered best practice. Segregated classrooms for disabled children were—and still are a reality. Sometimes they exist because individual students genuinely need one-on-one attention. But more often, they're a reflection of a deeper societal belief: that disabled and non-disabled children should not occupy the same spaces.

This segregation extends beyond the classroom. Disabled bodies are routinely excluded. Full inclusion is only now beginning to take shape in any meaningful way, and even then, attitudinal barriers remain deeply entrenched.

Did my parents know about the laws concerning my education? They knew about Brown v. Board of Education, but for them, the law didn't matter. I was a Doucette, and that meant I was going to school. No board was going to tell my parents, especially my mother, otherwise.

So, I had to go through competency testing.

My mother recalls one test that involved two boxes: one empty, the other holding an Ernie doll. A therapist asked, "Luticha, which box is empty?" I looked at the therapist, then at the boxes. Then I picked up the Ernie doll, pointed to its now-empty box, and said, "That one!"

While I am no Ruby Bridges, I understood, like her, what the assignment was. Even at a young age, I knew I carried the unfair burden of having to prove my humanity and worth just to get an education. There were no cameras or screaming mobs, but the same attitude prevailed.

I know so many disabled individuals from my generation and older who went through the same thing. Our struggle is often hidden, unacknowledged. We are not nameless faces, we are human beings with thoughts, feelings, and more.

My mother says she laughed so hard during the testing that she was kicked out. The administrators claimed she was creating bias and influencing my responses. At one point, they stormed out, exclaiming, "Mrs. Doucette, she's refusing to finger paint with tapioca!"

My mother replied, "What the hell does that have to do with her ability to go to school? I wouldn't finger paint with tapioca either. She just doesn't like getting her hands dirty."

The results showed I was ahead of my peers. Still, the board didn't want to set a precedent. I was "mainstreamed" with students my age; a term older disabled folks like me use to describe attending classes with our peers rather than being placed in Special Ed.

But as with many things, when you fight for a seat at the table, you often discover that the table is a hot mess express, full of chaos and incompetence. We fought so hard for me to access education, only to realize I wasn't actually being educated. Segregation, it seemed, was still the goal.

While I had a right to be educated, this did not necessarily include the right to participate in things like school trips. My mother had to fight for me to attend even those. The annual class trip was to Marine World Africa USA in Vallejo, California. To my six-year-old self, and to many school-aged children, that was the epitome, the Holy Grail, of surviving homework. And yet, I wasn't allowed to go. Instead, I was put into detention with other "unruly" kids, where I would sit and play make-believe with the ants in the ant farm in that particular hot and sticky classroom.

Recreational activities weren't really a thing in the '80s and '90s for disabled people in general, and especially not for disabled children. Accessible playgrounds were nonexistent, particularly in our small

Northern California town. Most programs revolved around models that nonprofits could bill to Medicaid. That's still largely the model, even in 2025.

While advocacy for accessible playgrounds and inclusive recreation has grown, these efforts are often deprioritized. Recreation sits at the intersection of privilege: Do you actually have the free time to seek out recreational opportunities? Class—do you have disposable income to access them? Racism, there's a long history of Black people being policed or excluded from public spaces, even as we created our own spaces for joy that were often deemed inferior. Sexism, recreation is seen as gendered (boys do x, girls do y). And ableism, is the space actually accessible?

So, your choices were limited. Maybe a restaurant, usually a chain, but prior to the Americans with Disabilities Act, even restaurants weren't accessible, and many still aren't today. Or the movie theater.

Thanks to the Rehabilitation Act, libraries were fully accessible. I don't remember learning to read, the words just somehow started making sense, but we often went to the library. My parents made a habit of living near one, a habit I still keep. My mother would take my older brother and me, pulling a red Radio Flyer wagon, and we were allowed to check out 21 books between the three of us. Many times, I'd take 19, and my brother and mother would split the rest.

My mom had one rule: it didn't matter if I finished all my books over the weekend, we were only going to the library once a week. If I finished early, I had to reread them. Through those books, I visited worlds I never knew existed, places that felt foreign or mysterious, and I went on adventures with characters who became friends. I too floated down the lazy river with Huck Finn on hot summer days in my bedroom. It wasn't just escapism, it was proof that something else existed beyond the tiny, confining world that the accident cosigned me into. And I began to believe that possibility was real.

So, I'd think about Huck Finn or Jo[Little Women] while watching the ants build in their little ant farm in that sticky classroom, while the rest of the kids enjoyed the sights and sounds of Marine World Africa USA.

But my mother didn't give up. She fought the school board so I could attend field trips like the other kids. And one day, I, too, boarded the loud yellow bus to finally see what all the fuss and hullabaloo was about!

Long story short, I didn't like it.

I wasn't allowed to see the sea lions with the rest of the class. They said my wheelchair would scare the animals. So, my mother took me around the park on our own. She had the bright idea of taking me to feed some of the animals. For just a few cents, you could buy an ice cream cone filled with feed and walk up onto a boardwalk to feed the giraffes.

Now, mind you, the only giraffe I'd ever seen was on a David Attenborough special. And to this day, I'm not great at judging size or scale, unless it's chemical structures. So, there I was, tiny, six years old, face to face with a massive mouth and a giant purple tongue looming toward me. Naturally, the only logical reaction was to scream, "It's going to eat me!"

Both my mother and the giraffe were bewildered. My mother swiftly wheeled me away as I sobbed, giraffe slobber coating the seed-stuffed ice cream cone. Through clenched teeth, she hissed, "You are embarrassing me!" She had worked so hard to get me there, only for me to cause a scene.

I think there's a deep lesson I've come to understand it's okay to work hard to reach a goal or try something new and then realize you don't like it. Too often, especially for children with disabilities and I know this from personal experience, we're not given the space to simply like or dislike things. There's this unspoken rule that once you've worked hard to access a space, saying "this isn't for me" is seen as ungrateful or even disrespectful to those who helped you get there.

But part of being human is having access to the full range of experiences. It's not just about what's good or bad, what you enjoy, or dislike helps shape who you are. Disabled people are often given a narrow definition of identity, one that's written into reports that can follow us for a lifetime. These narrow narratives can hinder our access to opportunities. We're frequently not allowed to grow, shift, or change our minds. It's ironic, given how often disabilities are labeled as "rigid." I've personally been accused of rigid thinking, but nothing feels more inflexible than a nonprofit that says you can only access specific services and if your needs fall outside of that, well, too bad. Or a life plan that tells you who you are based on one narrow interpretation, then limits your access based on that version of you.

I've made it a point to speak up when I don't like something, and also when I do. If I disliked something in the past but have since changed my mind, I let that be okay. That, to me, is part of aging and growing. It's a lesson I learned deeply, in the middle of a meltdown with my mom, tears flowing, clutching a soggy slobbery ice cream cone.

I've also become a fierce advocate for expanding recreational opportunities for disabled people. I've worked with a group to help make the Erie Canal more accessible and inclusive for kayaking and hand cycling. I've done outrigger canoe races with nondisabled friends (we wrote 'The Chicks That Kick" in red lipstick on our arms and frequently won in our category). I created a Leadership Academy for disabled youth, using sports to teach leadership and advocacy skills. I'm lucky to be part of Ludus Fencing Club, an inclusive space where the goal is simply to enjoy fencing. Sport is not just about going to the Olympics or Paralympics, sometimes, it's just about having fun.

And "just" is a word disabled people rarely get to use. There's usually so much red tape and advocating just to access the most basic spaces. So having opportunities here in Rochester, NY where you can simply go online, reserve an adaptive kayak or hand cycle, and show up knowing your access needs are met, that's extraordinary. Or going to a fencing class and knowing your coach will support you, however you show up, and genuinely wants you to have the best possible experience.

My public-school education didn't last long. Around age seven or eight (I can't remember exactly), my parents pulled my older brother and me out of school. My mom had been one of those parent volunteers who helped in the classroom, often grading papers. One day, the teacher told her, "Mrs. Doucette, you can't correct papers with a red pen." My mom, confused, asked why not. The teacher said, "Because it hurts their feelings."

My mom replied bluntly, "If they don't want their feelings hurt, they should get the answer right."

She was furious that we weren't being taught to spell properly. The teacher had said it was more about how the kids felt the word should be spelled. My mom said, "That's not real life. It's not about how you feel, it's about what is. The word 'enough' isn't spelled E-N-U-F. It's E-N-O-U-G-H. And no amount of feelings is going to change that."

So, they pulled us out, believing they could provide a better education, one rooted not only in academic excellence but also in Black history and cultural awareness. At that time, I was already reading at a collegiate level, and my mom was deeply concerned that my writing wasn't developing at the same pace.

And truly, what was the point of fighting for me to be included if they weren't going to do their jobs properly and educate me?

Looking back, I realize my parents taught me a valuable lesson, one they never stated outright: sometimes, it's okay to go your own way. They showed me that tools and resources exist outside the classroom, and that

I could access them. We spent countless hours at the library or exploring museums, learning about works of art and reading about the artists and their time periods using books we checked out. My parents encouraged me to ask questions and to read from multiple sources and perspectives so I could form my own opinions.

To this day, I ask questions. Living in the United States, where education, and science are under constant threat, I see critical thinking and inquiry as essential to moving forward. Not just asking why we're here, but how we got here and what it will take to build a future that truly includes everyone's humanity.

Even now, I work with parents and other disabled people who are navigating the very same issues I faced as a child. Disabled children still don't have equal access to education, or even the opportunity to live life on their own terms.

I often wonder: what does it take to push the needle toward liberation? How do we boldly say that what we had wasn't working, and that we must actively build the change we want to see in the world?

Today, I live a life I could only dream of during those warm summer days in that hot sticky detention classroom. It's a peaceful life. On a hot day, instead of floating along the Mississippi River in my imagination with Huck Finn, I might be kayaking down the Erie Canal, listening to an audiobook of his travels or relaxing with a cool drink on the rooftop of my apartment. That little girl who dreamed of adventure has had plenty.

I've hiked up an active volcano in Costa Rica with a group of other disabled people and even lost a boot while skydiving. These days, no one has to convince me to travel or seek out adventure. I've visited places like Hong Kong and Mexico and often go to Toronto to see friends. And when I need a dose of spontaneity, I simply hop in my car and drive to places unknown.

Acknowledgements

Shout out to me for becoming and living out my wildest dreams.

About the Author

Luticha is a veteran disability justice advocate who graduated from the Rochester Institute of Technology with a degree in Bioinformatics, where she developed protein surface prediction algorithms. Currently, Luticha lives as a free Black person and business owner in Rochester, NY. She is a graduate of the Leadership and Education in Neurodevelopmental Disabilities (LEND) Fellowship program, an AUCD Emerging Leader, an inductee into the Susan M. Daniels Disability Mentoring Hall of Fame established by the National Disability Mentoring Coalition, and the 2020–2021 Distinguished Alumni Awardee from the Rochester Institute of Technology.

Luticha's research and writing have been featured in various publications such as *Insect Molecular Biology, Toxicon, The New York Times*, and *Yes! Magazine*. She is the owner of Catalyst Consulting Associates, which helps organizations, leaders, and advocates examine themselves across race/racism, gender identity, and disability in policies, practices, procedures, and relationships. She's an avid indoor gardener, kayaker, and fencer.

How to Connect with Luticha:

LinkedIn: Luticha Andre Doucette
Facebook: @Luticha Andre Doucette
Instagram: @freedomofmovement35

LaKisha Maxey

Children's Author
Podcaster
Poet
Guest Speaker, Patient Advocacy Council Symposia Panel
Society for Medical Decision Making (SMDM) – 45th Annual North American Meeting

A Series of Unfortunate Events:
The Disabled Edition

By Any Means Necessary: A Bronx Morning

I woke up that morning with sunlight stretched across my chest, as if the rays were reaching for my face. The sun felt like a silent promise of a good day ahead.

I called my BFF/travel assistant/personal care patient—aka my mother—to remind her to be ready to leave on time. I sang along to my favorite song in the shower and even did a little dance while getting dressed. For the day's outfit, I intentionally chose a loose-fitting T-shirt and stretchy leggings—comfort over everything.

Then came the AFO foot brace. It essentially gives my leg the structure it needs so it doesn't buckle, preventing me from collapsing to the floor. It also lifts the toes of my affected foot to keep me from tripping as I walk. That's the challenge of living with drop foot—a condition marked by difficulty, or even inability, in lifting the front part of the foot. Without my brace, the risk is real: dragging toes, tripping, and falling. And honestly, I've had enough falls to last a lifetime.

I made my way down the stairs, one step at a time, grabbed my pink walker, and stepped outside to wait for the rideshare. I plopped into my father's lopsided plastic lawn chair outside my parents' first-floor window, ignoring the industrial chain and padlock that tethered the chair to the window guard.

Why all the extra security, you ask? I live in the Bronx! It's essential to secure your belongings at all times. Besides, MacGyver Maxey, aka my father, has subconsciously customized our home in such a way that if anyone ever tried to break in, it would be like a real-life Home Alone scene. They'd be met with a tangled mess of electrical tape, twine, and old telephone cords, just a few of Dad's many creative DIY tools.

But it's more than just makeshift security. It's a symbol. Every twist of tape, every extension cord, is a visual reminder of my father's relentless commitment to protecting his family. He safeguards what he loves, by any means necessary. Every time I spot a screw or cord, I see love. My dad is my hero.

The Urban Porch

So back to the story. I sat in my father's chair waiting for my mother to finally come outside so we could leave. The chair I was sitting in is located right outside of our house, behind the gate. It's the urban equivalent of a porch. You know—you can keep an eye on the neighbors, learn what's going on in the neighborhood, and follow strangers with your eyes to see their comings and goings.

The familiar sounds of the Bronx morning surrounded me: the distant hum of traffic on the Grand Concourse, the rhythmic clatter of the elevated train, children's voices echoing from the schoolyard down the block. These sounds had become my morning symphony, a reminder that life continued its steady pulse around me, even when mine had been so dramatically altered.

The rideshare finally arrived, and my mom and I made it to the doctor's office. So far, today was a good day, and I was ready for my MRI.

Ever since my stroke in 2020, because of all the damage and changes it caused in my body, I have several doctors who schedule me for annual blood work, x-rays, MRIs, CT scans, and—okay, I'm exaggerating about the anal probes, but sometimes I feel just as violated. Basically, they're looking for any potential problems or changes in my health. Physical, occupational, and speech therapy have helped immensely over the years. They helped me unlearn how I used to do things and relearn how I can do them now. I had to learn, and I am still learning how to live and function in this new body.

For instance, the right side of my body has weakness, stiffness, partial paralysis, and spasticity. My right arm is usually curled toward my chest, and my hand is in a ball. My quarterly Botox injections help loosen the muscles, but not 100%. My trigger point injections help with shoulder pain, and the cortisone injections help with hip pain. My brain has not "recognized" my right arm or leg yet, so they still feel like they weigh a ton. The AFO foot brace is about ten pounds by itself.

Without the AFO foot brace, I drag my right foot when I walk, and I circumduct my leg because my right hip, thigh, and ankle are stiff and weak, and I can't bend the knee. With the AFO foot brace, walking is much easier, but I still circumduct. Most of the pain in my body comes from atrophy of joints and muscles I can't or hardly use since the stroke, or from inflammation in my body.

And oh, my toes are curled under on my right side, so if I don't trim my toenails, I sound like a wild animal walking across my wooden floors—ready to use her claws to eat me and feed her young. One day I'll tell you the story of the time it took three nail technicians to do my pedicure on one foot. Definitely a top-five embarrassing moment.

The Appointment

Back to the story. Today's scheduled appointment was for an MRI. At the doctor's office, a technician called my name while standing at the double doors with an inviting smile. She nodded as I approached and guided me to the changing room. After changing, I walked past the waiting area and headed toward the procedure room.

Let me share a post-stroke hack I learned during my ninety days in rehabilitation, following four days in the hospital after my stroke. During the day, the staff always insisted I wear my leg brace and sneakers, even though I was in a wheelchair, for liability reasons, of course. But at night, before bed, they required me to wear hospital-issued socks with a sticky grip on the bottom. This was to provide traction in case I got out of my wheelchair and attempted to go to the restroom alone, reducing the risk of slipping and falling.

Remember, I have drop foot, and the muscles in my ankle are weak. When I walk, I tend to drag my foot. The trick I discovered is to turn the sock upside down, placing the non-sticky part on the sole and the sticky part on top. When I'm not wearing my leg brace at home and I try walking without circumducting, the upside-down sock helps. The soft side of the sock glides across the floor more easily, allowing me to move more naturally. It's a coping mechanism I had to learn, one of many small adaptations that have now become as natural as breathing.

The Symphony of Struggle

Back to the smiling technician, who was still patiently holding the door open. As I started walking, my underwear began to slip down. Step, slide, drag. Step, slide, drag. That was the rhythm playing in my head during this very personal calamity. It matched my left-foot step, the slide of my undies, and my unbraced right leg dragging behind (I couldn't wear the brace for the MRI procedure).

It was like a whole symphony playing in my head as I walked. Boom, boop, shhhh. Step, slide, drag. The internal noise was so loud I couldn't concentrate on the technician, who was talking the whole time. I heard nothing. I just grinned and nodded. The technician kept smiling as she now held open the second door leading to the actual procedure room.

I left my pink walker outside and was assisted onto the table. That part was awkward, by now, my underwear had slid down to thigh level, but I managed.

As many of you know, an MRI is hell for people who are claustrophobic. You're slid into a tight, straw-like tube and subjected to loud, scary clicking and beeping as the machine scans your brain.

Usually, to keep my mind occupied during the fifteen to twenty minutes inside, I pray, worship God, compose my grocery list, sing songs for which I only know half the lyrics and half the tune, anything to pass the time. But today, I already had a pressing topic in mind: how to get back to the changing room with my underwear still intact.

I came up with several plans, weighed the pros, cons, and hazards of each, and was ready to execute.

The Unraveling

When the MRI was over, the technician adjusted my sock—sticky side down—smiled, and said, "There you go!"

In my head, I screamed, "NO!" But I was too embarrassed to stop her. Refusing the sock correction would've meant explaining why I needed it upside down, which would have triggered one of my new insecurities: becoming the topic of conversation among strangers and drawing more attention to the deficiencies of my body—and my new workarounds.

This vulnerability is uncomfortable. It often forces me to ask for or accept help—something this extremely independent woman still hasn't fully gotten used to. So, I said nothing and let the technician feel like she was being helpful.

Before I got off the table, my airtight escape plan was ruined, and I had to go rogue. I quickly grabbed the side of my thigh-level undies through the gown and pulled them up with my unaffected left hand.

Leaving the MRI room wasn't too hard. Sure, I had to perform a low-height roundhouse karate kick to walk, because the sticky side of the sock was now face down, and I couldn't slide my foot across the linoleum floor. But I managed.

Everything seemed to be working, and I heaved a sigh of relief.

The technician guided me back to my pink walker in the hallway, then returned to the procedure room. I took a deep breath and began executing my new plan—Plan B. After all, the changing room was right there.

The Walk of Shame

Those legendary twenty paces have earned the top spot as the most embarrassing moment of my life. Holding up my underwear with my left hand, I used my affected right arm to reach for my walker. Lying inside the freezing MRI machine had left my body stiff and my joints locked, even after just a few moments. So, when I tried to grab the handle of the walker, I realized my hand was frozen into a tight fist—I couldn't open it.

Unfortunately, this happens pretty often. It's due to spasticity and the weakness in the muscles of my fingers and hand. The curling of my arm is my body's way of protecting itself. During the stroke, my body literally defended itself by curling up into a ball. How amazing is that?

Unable to extend my fingers to grasp the walker's handle, I had no choice but to navigate using my clenched fist.

It was now obvious that I'd have to swiftly move to Plan C. The goal remained the same: get to the changing room with both my underwear and my walker. So I began my journey in the only position that seemed feasible, holding my underwear (which had by now slipped to my knees) with my left hand, using my outstretched right arm, with my hand still balled up, to guide the walker, and walking with my left knee slightly bent so it could help push the walker forward. And of course, I couldn't forget the low-height roundhouse kick-walk I had to do to clear the sock grippies.

I was making my way to the changing room, feeling slightly ridiculous, but successful, nonetheless. The hallway felt longer than usual, each step was a calculated effort to preserve what little dignity I had left. The fluorescent lights buzzed overhead, casting that harsh, unforgiving glow only medical facilities seem to perfect.

Then I reached the second door past the procedure room, the one that led to the waiting room.

The Moment of Truth

I had made it this far, right? I figured I was in the home stretch. With a tight fist full of fury, I grabbed the doorknob and twisted it sharply to the right. Because I was gripping it with a balled fist, I thought I'd need a little extra strength to keep the slick metal from slipping away. I leaned in, using my body weight to push the door open.

It worked, a little too well.

I stumbled forward as the door flung open unexpectedly and clumsily tumbled into the waiting room. Then I stopped dead in my tracks.

Remember the Mannequin Challenge? The one where you strike a funny frozen pose with friends, and whoever moves first loses? That's exactly what I looked like, mid-stride, frozen in place. There were only two other people in the room, all of us wearing gowns. Both of them stared at me: one was an older gentleman, the other a woman in her twenties.

In my mind, if I stayed still, maybe they wouldn't really see me. And more importantly—maybe they wouldn't see what had just happened.

Somewhere between the door and my grand entrance, I had lost grip of my underwear. It now rested in a pitiful circle around my ankles.

The silence was deafening.

The air conditioning unit hummed from the corner—apparently the only thing brave enough to break the awkward quiet. I could feel the heat rush to my face, that now-familiar flush of mortification I'd become all too acquainted with since my stroke.

Plan D

At this point, what does one do? Any reaction would have drawn even more attention to me, as if standing there with my underwear around my ankles wasn't already enough of a spectacle.

For a few minutes, it felt like everyone in the waiting room had frozen mid-movement, like they were playing the mannequin challenge: their eyes locked on my feet, mouths slightly open in stunned silence; me, staring down at my fallen underwear with sadness, disappointment, and betrayal clouding my eyes.

I now considered Plan D.

I took a deep breath, lifted my head, and shuffled toward the changing room. I did a sort of low-height, round-house kick-walk, clutching my walker with one good hand and curling the other into a fist. And yes, my underwear still around my ankles.

I had to pretend no one was watching.

With my chin held high, I moved past the people in the waiting room, the nurses walking by, and the receptionist behind the desk. All eyes were on me. Still, I pressed on toward the changing room as if I were walking back to my seat after receiving an Oscar.

But once I made it there, I fell apart.

I wasn't just crying, I was weeping. Weeping from embarrassment, frustration, betrayal, and grief.

Grieving the person who could once walk swiftly from the procedure room to the changing room in three seconds. Grieving the version of myself I had lost and in this moment, hating the version that remained.

The changing room felt smaller than before, its walls seeming to close in around me as I sat on the small bench, shoulders shaking under the weight of everything I had lost.

A simple twenty-foot walk had become an insurmountable challenge; a painful reminder of how drastically my world had shrunk to fit this new reality.

The Aftermath

The story ends just as expected. I made it to the changing room, immediately tossed my underwear into the trash, and dressed in my clothes. When I stepped out, there were stares, whispers, and laughter. But they all hit the soundproof wall I had built in my mind since the stroke, brick by brick, event by event. It was the only way I knew to push through the trauma.

One of the most important things I had to learn was that, in order to heal, I needed to shut out the world and focus entirely on myself. So, at that moment, I fixed my eyes on a single point in the near distance: a basic, mundane watercolor painting, the kind you find in every hospital waiting room or doctor's office. I stared straight ahead, walked slowly, and made my way right out the door, where my patient mother waited in the general seating area.

She could see in my eyes that I wasn't okay, but I'd never admit it to her. She's been my superhero all my life. But now, as she grows older, she looks to me to be strong, her superhero. And I'm here for that. So, despite the hurt and the embarrassment, I gathered myself, helped my mom up, called a rideshare, and went back home, where I cried across my bed in the dark.

Finding Light Through Laughter

That incident happened almost four years ago. I called several friends to tell them what had happened, and I got the response I expected: they all laughed. Belly laughs. Tearful laughs.

How horrible must it have felt to have close friends laugh at such an embarrassing and traumatic experience?

No. Their laughter is my therapy.

It's a reminder that, despite seeing the changes in myself, my close friends refuse to make me feel like they see me any differently. My body has been through trauma, from my curled toes to my brain, which now suffers from aphasia.

Before, I used to cry every day thinking about everything I've lost, and everyone I've lost, because they couldn't handle my changes. I cried because my beautiful handwriting is gone, and I'm now forced to write left-handed with the penmanship of a third-grader. I cried because the mirror shows me the droop on the right side of my mouth, and sometimes I can't stop drooling.

Maybe it's just me, and I'm a little weird, but their laughter reminds me that even though I used to grieve the old Kisha every day, my friends still see me as the same Kisha.

And that makes me feel like my old self.

Faith as Foundation

Psalm 30:5 KJV says, "For his anger endureth but a moment; in his favour is life: weeping may endure for a night, but joy cometh in the morning." Joy didn't come the first morning after the stroke. In fact, it took almost two years for me to feel joy again. I've learned how and where to find my happiness.

I'll drink hot tea even in the middle of the summer because it feels like a warm hug inside my belly. I'll rewatch *Law & Order: SVU* because now that I've seen every episode of every season, I can focus on other things. Like, how many times has Benson changed her hairstyle? Or why did Stabler just disappear after season twelve? Anything to keep my mind occupied from the deep, dark place that I often found myself in. That show is my security blanket. I told my therapist I watch it as a happy distraction.

In fact, my youngest son has learned that whenever he sees me wrapped in a blanket on the couch watching Law & Order: SVU, it's a sign that Mom is either slipping into depression or already there. My oldest son picks up on it too, he'll often send my grandson upstairs to cheer up Gigi. And it works. My grandson brings me joy. My family brings me joy. My friends and loved ones bring me joy. But my deepest joy comes from God.

John 15:9-11 NIV says, "As the Father has loved me, so have I loved you. Now remain in my love. If you keep my commands, you will remain in my love, just as I have kept my Father's commands and remain in his love. I have told you this so that my joy may be in you and that your joy may be complete."

You will never find joy in the mirror. The mirror shows you the body that betrayed you. You can't find joy in your friends. You'll end up jealous of their lives and the life you think you can no longer have. You won't find joy in your family. You may feel like a burden to them or overwhelmed by their needs you can't satisfy. You will slip into the darkness. Spiral into depression. You will hit rock bottom.

Until you start to pray. Don't pray for answers; pray for peace. Pray for clarity. Every day that goes by, I tell God I can't do life without Him. With God, my body didn't betray me. Instead, she saved me from a fate worse than the one I received, or even death. With God, I can be proud of my friends' accomplishments, and they can celebrate mine. With God, I pray for assistance and resources, and I'm not ashamed to admit I'm on psychotropics until I'm strong enough on my own. With God, the joy I feel comes from remembering I am His daughter, He loves me, and He saved me to serve Him.

Learning to Live Again

Everything is different for me now. All the two-handed, right-hand-dominant activities that once felt so natural, I've had to relearn using only one hand, and not even my dominant one.

Brushing my teeth. Styling my hair. Even something like putting my hair in a ponytail requires me to lean my head against a wall just to get it done. It's another coping mechanism I've had to develop.

At dinnertime, I can't just grab my plate and cup and head to the table in one go. I carry my plate first, then return for my cup. When I'm out with friends, I can't walk around sipping coffee or enjoying an ice cream cone. And if it's raining, I can't carry an umbrella. I need my cane in my left, unaffected, hand to keep steady. My right hand is still too weak and shaky to carry hot drinks or anything with even a little weight.

Stairs are another challenge. If there's no banister on the left side, I have to grip the right-side rail with my left hand and go up sideways. And when I'm cooking, I have to be extremely careful. If my right hand touches a hot pot, I might not even realize it until I smell burning flesh, thanks to the numbness and decreased sensitivity that also affect that side.

Yes, everything is different for me now. Even opening a jar has become a two-person job. Getting dressed in the morning requires strategic planning. Something as small as putting on earrings takes deliberate coordination.

But each small victory, buttoning a shirt, applying makeup with my left hand, or making it up a flight of stairs on my own, feels like conquering a mountain.

The Gift of Perspective

Going back to the betrayal of my undies, I can laugh at that story now. It's my go-to tale at get-togethers. It's my most requested.

"Hey, Keesh, tell the story where your underpants ended up on the floor."

And I always think, Well, you already ruined the punchline.

That story now represents, for me, the series of unfortunate events that became my healing journey. You think you have your future mapped out (like intentionally choosing your outfit for the day), but life shifts (like my undies), you try to adjust (Plans A, B, and C), and in the end, you have to pray, take a deep breath, and let God lead you (just like I made it back to the changing room and to my mother).

Those words can be said in 0.2 seconds, but it took me years to figure that out. I'm still figuring it out. My mental and emotional breakdowns went from every day to every month or so. I have my triggers. Watching a young man run for a taxi makes me cry, remembering when I used to run for taxis. Seeing the happy nuptials of strangers in a magazine makes me wonder if I'll ever find that kind of happiness now that I'm disabled.

Maybe one day I'll stop breaking down altogether. But sometimes, I still grieve for the old Kisha. And grief never disappears; it just becomes manageable. So until I'm strong enough to stop pitying myself, or brave enough to push past my fears and doubts, I'll follow 2 Corinthians 12:9 (NIV):

"But he said to me, 'My grace is sufficient for you, for my power is made perfect in weakness.'

Therefore, I will boast all the more gladly about my weaknesses, so that Christ's power may rest on me."

I fight hard every day to remind myself that although I'm still weak on the outside, my joy and strength on the inside come from God. And as long as He wakes me up every day, He's giving me another opportunity to grow stronger and keep praising Him.

The underwear incident taught me that dignity isn't about never falling down, it's about how you choose to get back up. It's about finding the courage to walk with your head held high, even when your underwear is around your ankles. It's about discovering that sometimes the most embarrassing moments become the most transformative, and that healing often comes disguised as humiliation.

Most importantly, it taught me that I'm not defined by my limitations, but by my limitless capacity to adapt, overcome, and find joy in the journey, no matter how many times my underwear decides to stage a rebellion.

Acknowledgments

Thank you to my friends and family for your constant motivation and inspiration.

Zoe, I think you laughed the hardest when I first told you this story, so it's no surprise you suggested it for this anthology. Thank you for the push.

Lots of love to the friends I communicate with every day. I can always count on you for encouragement, hangout invites, deep confessions, 3 a.m. chats, and about 101 miscellaneous topics that keep me laughing, thinking, and entertained.

Nsenga, not a day goes by that I don't miss you. If I had known I wouldn't have you to do life with, I would've cherished every moment even more. You'd be proud—just like we planned. I sat on the porch, in a rocking chair, drinking sweet tea. The wind was still, but the dreamcatcher danced for two whole minutes. I know, sis. I love you and miss you too.

To my parents, Derek, Dalen, and Sage: when my cup is empty, you fill me up. And when yours is empty, I fill you up.

Sage—Gigi continues to get better for you.

To my new publisher, Kebra Moore: a Facebook group connected us, but your love for God and your amazing personality are what truly kept me. And your six degrees of separation from my cousin LaShay didn't hurt either. Thank you for your patience and understanding. Representation matters and seeing you succeed gives me the courage to keep going.

About the Author

LaKisha Maxey is the author of two powerful books released in September 2023—*A Stroke at Midnight: Poetry for the Journey from Trauma to Healing* and *Wheels Like Me*, a children's book. Both works were inspired by a life-altering stroke LaKisha suffered in August 2020. Through her passion and love for writing, she found a pathway to healing and now uses her words to help others heal emotionally and psychologically. She is currently working on her next writing project.

LaKisha is currently pursuing a graduate degree in Psychology, with an expected completion date of 2025–2026. She holds a bachelor's degree in Business with a concentration in Human Resources Management. With over twenty years of experience in customer service, including training, mentoring, and coaching, LaKisha brings a wealth of professional insight to her work.

She also dedicated a decade to homeless services, where she conducted one-on-one mediation, crisis intervention, conflict resolution, and behavioral assessments with shelter residents. Her responsibilities included both in-person and telephone assessments for program eligibility, as well as organizing social events to promote healthy relationships between residents and staff.

LaKisha is now retired from the United States Federal Government.

As an author, poet, and stroke survivor, LaKisha has embarked on a mission to raise awareness about stroke and its emotional aftermath. She is now a dedicated stroke awareness advocate and has been featured on podcasts such as *No More Chains* with host Shawn Cornelius and *Poetry for Black Girls* with Angelina, where she shared how writing became a vital part of her recovery.

LaKisha's literary journey continues with her upcoming release, *Wheels Like Us*, part of the *Wheels Like Me* series, along with a host of other creative and writing projects on the horizon.

How to Connect with LaKisha:

LinkedIn: LaKisha Maxey
Facebook: @LaKisha Maxey
Instagram: @lovebecomesherwords

Keisha Belcher

NC License Real Estate Broker
CEO of Auxiliary Beauty Consultants, LLC
Active member of The Order of the Eastern Stars
NC-Licensed Cosmetologist
Multiple Sclerosis and NMO, team leader of walk MS

The Journey of the Spine in My Eyes!

The First Shadow

On a February morning in 2005, I woke up, got dressed, and began preparing my daughter for school. As I moved around the house gathering what I needed before dropping her off, I noticed a very irritating sensation in my right eye, like an eyelash was stuck in it. Like anyone would, I rubbed my eye and tugged gently at my lashes, hoping to stop the discomfort.

Even as I drove my daughter to school, the irritation persisted. I kept rubbing and pulling on my lashes as the feeling grew more intense. After dropping her off, I started my drive back home.

But during the drive, I realized that my right eye had started to blur. My fiancé had taken the day off work, which was unusual unless he had an appointment or something important to attend to. In hindsight, I believe it was God's will that he was home when I returned.

By the time I pulled into the driveway and got out of the car, my vision in the right eye had vanished completely. Panic set in. I stumbled into the house, where he stood waiting for me. I let out a panicked scream. As he turned to look at me, I collapsed to my knees, crying and shouting, "I can't see! I can't see anything out of my right eye!"

He calmly and gently knelt beside me, lifted me up, and held me close as I sobbed in fear and confusion. "Kee," he whispered, "It's okay. Everything will be fine."

I know in my heart that God made sure he was home with me that day because I needed him more than ever. He said, "Let's schedule an appointment with an eye doctor. I'm sure everything will be okay."

We called a few clinics before finally finding one that could see me the same day. On the way there, I was overwhelmed with panic. My mind raced as I sat in the car unable to see. When I covered my left eye with my hand, the complete darkness in my right eye intensified my fear.

After a thorough examination, the eye doctor told me he couldn't find anything that would explain my complete vision loss. His recommendation? Get some eyeglasses. Looking back, it was a ridiculous suggestion, one that made no sense at all. Still, I bought the glasses.

A few days later, my vision began to return. I breathed a deep sigh of relief and thanked God. But a month later, the nightmare returned, this time in my left eye. Once again, I was blind, only now in the opposite eye.

My fiancé took me to a different eye doctor. I explained what had happened before, how the previous doctor couldn't explain my vision loss and had prescribed glasses that I clearly didn't need.

The second doctor examined me carefully, then looked up and said, "From my perspective, I can't find any explanation for this vision loss. But it could possibly be MS."

I stared at him blankly and thought, in complete ignorance, What the fuck is MS?

The only thing that came to mind was Jerry Lewis and the childhood memories of his televised marathons raising money for muscular dystrophy. I had never heard of MS before. I sat there confused and uneducated about what he was talking about.

He went on to explain that MS stood for Multiple Sclerosis and that I needed to see a neurologist. He then referred me to what was, at the time, Carolina's Medical Neurology.

God was undoubtedly working in my favor, although I hadn't realized it at the time. My neurologist, Dr. Michael Kaufman, who happened to be the head of the entire neurology department, took charge of my case. After our first appointment, he ordered a series of tests, including blood work and an MRI. While we anxiously awaited the results, he started me on a seven-day IV steroid infusion, followed by a ten-day taper pack.

When the MRI results came back, I remember him looking slightly taken aback. The scan revealed a few very vague lesions on my brain. He and I sat down and discussed a treatment plan, which I began immediately.

Between 2005 and 2007, I tried every available medication for multiple sclerosis (MS), but none provided relief. In fact, my symptoms seemed to be worsening—becoming more aggressive with time. By early 2007, I had lost vision in my right eye so frequently that I could no longer see peripherally. New symptoms began to surface, including numbness and tingling in my lower extremities, persistent lower back pain, and the sensation of a tight band wrapping around my torso. Through it all, the only thing that brought temporary relief was a seven-day IV steroid infusion.

One Saturday morning, my then-husband dropped me off at work, where I rented a salon suite. I had a full day of clients scheduled. After unlocking the door and prepping my station, I greeted my first client and began draping her while we discussed her service. As I walked her to the shampoo area, I started to feel nauseous but pushed through, determined to keep the day moving.

We returned to the suite, and as she sat down in the chair, I suddenly rushed to the trash can and began vomiting uncontrollably. When I looked up, I saw my husband walking through the door, another stylist had called him to let him know I wasn't feeling well. He immediately took me to the nearest emergency room.

By the time we arrived and checked in, I had begun to lose central vision in my right eye. I ended up spending my 32nd birthday in the hospital, undergoing a seven-day IV steroid treatment. By the end of the week, my central vision had returned.

However, over the next few months, April, May, June, and July, I was hospitalized repeatedly for steroid infusions, as I continued losing vision in my eyes, though never in both at once. During this period, I also began experiencing new symptoms that caused severe pain and discomfort throughout my body. It was all still very new and overwhelming, for both me and my family.

I could tell that my neurologist was deeply concerned about what was happening to my body neurologically, especially since none of the MS medications seemed to help. I recall that when I became his patient in 2005, he had been planning to retire within a couple of years. However, he was so perplexed and troubled by my case that he postponed his retirement.

Looking back, I now realize that I wasn't very vocal or expressive about the intense physical pain I had begun to experience. In hindsight, I was in denial about what was happening to my health. I had always been healthy. There had never been anything I couldn't do physically, and I had never experienced the level of pain that was now spreading throughout my body.

In mid-August of that year, on a Sunday afternoon, my husband and I took our children to one of the larger malls in the area to begin school shopping. I remember it as if it happened yesterday. As we walked through the mall, I was experiencing excruciating pain in my lower back. Normally, I enjoyed school shopping even more than the kids did. But on that day, it took everything in me to mask how awful I was feeling. I didn't want to ruin our family outing by complaining about pain they couldn't help me with.

As the kids went in and out of the stores, I started asking them to go ahead while I waited on the benches just outside. Toward the end of our shopping trip, my cell phone rang. The caller ID displayed "MS Center." I remember thinking, Why would I be getting a call from them on a Sunday?

I answered, and it was Dr. Kaufman on the other end. He asked how I was feeling. I told him I was fine, all the while knowing my lower back felt like it was on fire. He responded, "You can't be fine, according to the MRI of your spine that I'm looking at."

In that moment, I wanted to scream and cry, not from pain, but because someone finally saw that I was not okay without me having to say it. Dr. Kaufman told me to go home, pack a bag, and meet him at the main hospital. He was going to admit me.

Once I arrived, he explained that the MRI showed several long lesions, scars, on my lower spine. Suddenly, everything made sense. That explained the unbearable lower back pain I'd been experiencing.

After I was admitted, he ordered a seven-day series of plasmapheresis, also known as therapeutic plasma exchange. This procedure removes, treats, and returns or replaces a patient's blood plasma. A machine separates the blood into red blood cells, white blood cells, platelets, and plasma. The plasma is then discarded and replaced with either synthetic plasma or plasma from a human donor.

During my first procedure, my body had an allergic reaction to the human donor plasma, so I was switched to synthetic plasma instead. After the seven days of treatment, I did begin to feel better and was finally released to go home.

Descending Into Darkness

In October, I began experiencing pain in my right eye. I knew that pain was often a sign that my vision would begin to deteriorate. I was already blind in the periphery of that eye, and by the time I was able to reach my doctor and get to his office, I had lost central vision as well. Despite being hospitalized and treated with IV steroids and plasmapheresis, the damage was irreversible. The optic nerve in my right eye had been severely compromised, and I was told I would never regain vision in that eye.

So, there I sat on the side of the hospital bed, waiting to be discharged, just after being told of my new reality: a life with vision in only one eye. My worst fear was coming true. And in that moment, my deepest fear wasn't just the physical loss, but being deemed and labeled as disabled. I was mentally and emotionally distraught. The ride home felt like the longest and quietest ride of my life; you could have heard a pin drop.

For the next few weeks, I found myself on a relentless emotional roller coaster, swinging from rage to heartbreak, devastation, and deep grief. One minute I had been a perfectly healthy, active woman and the next, I was classified as disabled. Everyone around me began treating me differently, as if that label defined me. I had always been independent, outgoing, and determined. And I was still a newlywed; I had just gotten married that January. The feelings of inadequacy as a woman, mother, and wife were gut-wrenching. The thought of not being able to continue thriving in my career as a cosmetologist and makeup artist left me devastated. As much love and support as I had around me, nothing could silence the mental and emotional turmoil that wreaked havoc on my well-being.

I remember that R. Kelly was on tour and performing in my city on Sunday, October 31st. My husband had bought us tickets, and for the first time in weeks, I felt genuinely excited. That morning, though, I noticed something strange, the tips of my fingers felt like they were buzzing. It was a tingling sensation I had never experienced before. As the day went on, the tingling became more intense, spreading further down my fingers. I chose not to tell my husband; afraid he might cancel our long-awaited night out.

We arrived at the concert with two other couples. If you know anything about R. Kelly's shows, you know they're impossible to sit still through, hit after hit, he kept the energy high. I didn't sit down once. I stood, sang, danced, and clapped along with the music. But during all of it, that same tingling sensation intensified, now coursing through the palms of my hands and fingers.

As the concert ended and we began walking to our cars, I noticed a strange sensation in my legs, and a dull pain started to settle in my lower back. Yet again, I chose not to mention any of the discomfort I had experienced throughout the day to my husband. We drove straight home because it was getting late, and he had to be up by 5 a.m. for work the next day.

I vividly remember waking up sometime in the early morning to use the restroom. As I returned to bed, I glanced at the alarm clock on his nightstand but couldn't make out the numbers. I stood in the darkness at the bathroom door, trying my best to see the time. All I could see was a red blur, no numbers, just red light. I walked over to his side of the bed to get closer, but still, the numbers remained unreadable. In that moment, I knew something was terribly wrong, I was losing vision in my left eye. It was the first time I realized I was starting to lose sight in both eyes at the same time.

Immediately, I woke my husband in a panic and told him my vision was fading in what had been my "good" eye. I needed to go to the emergency room. He sprang into action, got dressed, helped me get dressed, and drove to the hospital like a bat out of hell. After being registered and placed in a room, we anxiously waited for the ER doctor. Both of us repeatedly asked the medical staff to contact my neurologist.

Lying in that small ER room, I fixated on my husband's face as he stood beside me, holding my hand. I tried desperately not to blink because his face was slowly fading before me. I thought, *What if I never see his face again?* I wanted to remember every detail. When I finally told him I couldn't see him anymore, I could hear the panic in his voice as he called out to the medical staff, pleading for help. I then began trying to picture the faces of our children, fearing I might never see them again either.

Eventually, one of the on-call doctors contacted my neurologist, who happened to be the head of the neurology department. I lay there, listening to the frantic activity around me, nurses and doctors rushing in and out, trying to determine what had caused me to go completely blind in both eyes so suddenly.

By the time a nurse returned to inform us that my neurologist was on his way, a new symptom had emerged: my left arm began to feel heavy, as though it was no longer a part of me. It was a strange and alarming sensation I had never experienced before. I told my husband and the staff that it felt like dead weight.

When my neurologist, Dr. Kaufman, arrived, I had already been admitted to the hospital. The moment I heard his voice as he walked into the room, I said, "Dr. Kaufman, I can't move my left arm." While I had grasped the fact that I was now blind, it hadn't fully registered that the heaviness in my arm meant I was also experiencing paralysis.

Dr. Kaufman came to my bedside and began examining me while asking a series of questions about my arm. I asked if there was any medication he could give me to relieve the weighty feeling. He gently explained that there was no medication to ease that sensation. He told me that the signals from my brain that control movement in my arm, hand, and fingers were not connecting, that was why I couldn't move them. That was the moment I fully understood the severity of what was happening to my body and my vision.

Dr. Kaufman then explained that when I was previously admitted to a hospital closer to the salon where I had worked in March of that year, my lab work had been sent to the Mayo Clinic. The Mayo Clinic is a private academic medical center known for integrated healthcare, advanced research, and medical education. According to U.S. News & World Report, they hold more number-one rankings than any other hospital in the country and specialize in diagnosing and treating complex medical conditions.

My case had indeed proven to be a challenge, not just for Dr. Kaufman, but for the team of doctors he consulted. It had become clear that I did not have Multiple Sclerosis. By then, no lesions had been detected on my brain. Although I had been experiencing symptoms similar to those associated with MS, my condition had not responded to any of the treatments or therapies typically used for the various forms of MS.

Divine Revelation and Healing

Dr. Kaufman began to explain that my test results had come back from the Mayo Clinic, and there was finally a name for the unpredictable, monstrous, and debilitating condition I had been battling. I was diagnosed with Neuromyelitis Optica Spectrum Disorder (NMOSD), also known as Devic's disease, a rare autoimmune disorder that causes inflammation of the spinal cord and optic nerves.

It is a demyelinating condition, meaning the protective myelin sheaths surrounding nerve fibers are damaged, which prevents nerves from conducting electrical impulses properly. This autoimmune response causes the body to attack its own cells, primarily affecting the spinal cord and the optic nerves that connect the retina to the brain.

Neuromyelitis Optica is often misdiagnosed as multiple sclerosis (MS) or mistaken as a subtype of it. However, NMO is a distinct and separate condition.

In fact, the medications I had previously been given for MS were actually making the NMO more aggressive in my case. Finally, things began to make medical sense to my neurologist. He immediately devised a plan of action to treat the condition and help preserve my quality of life.

As the first day of being completely blind and paralyzed slowly came to an end, and my concerned and distraught family members began to leave, I found myself consoling and reassuring them that everything would be okay. In that moment, I couldn't explain or understand why I wasn't the one who was distraught or in need of comfort. I just remember feeling a stillness, both around me and within me, that brought a sense of peace.

There I lay, unable to see anything, unable to move my arm or hand. Yet I hadn't cried, screamed, or shown the emotional response everyone seemed to be waiting for.

That first night, I had a dream.

In my dream, I vividly remember looking up at the sky, where the clouds appeared as soft, pure-white cotton balls. Slowly, they began to separate from the center, revealing an illuminating light that shone directly down on me. Then I saw the face of the Lord, Jesus Christ, so clearly. I asked Him, "God, is this my time? Have you come to take me home to be with You?"

He responded, "No, it is not your time, My child. I have come to let you know, do not let your heart be weary, because this is not your battle. Stand firm in your faith in Me no matter what, and I've got you and everything and everyone directly connected to you."

When I woke up the next morning, I clearly understood why I had been so calm the day before. It was the God within me who had kept my mind and spirit at peace in the midst of the greatest storm I had ever faced in my life up to that point. I fully understood the assignment: to stand firm in my faith in God, no matter what the circumstances looked or felt like. I was to trust Him with all my heart, even when I didn't understand His plans for me. I realized that my life was no longer about the plans I had made for myself. Instead, I understood that God was going to use me for the greater good, according to His purpose for my life.

I did regain full vision in my left eye, and thankfully, the paralysis I experienced was not permanent. However, the battle to overcome the odds of such a rare and unfamiliar disorder had only just begun. And yet, after spending the entire decade of my thirties in and out of hospitals, I knew the battle had already been won. As I continued to grow and mature in my walk with God, I began to speak and declare that I would spend the decade of my forties walking in healing and living life to the fullest.

In March 2025, I was blessed to reach the milestone age of fifty. I am deeply and graciously grateful to be able to share my testimony with others while advocating, educating, and fundraising for research that could be a game-changer in the pursuit of a cure for what is currently known as a debilitating and incurable disorder.

Acknowledgements

I would like to graciously and gratefully thank my family and friends for their unwavering support throughout my journey. To my mother—who has always encouraged me and believed that I could achieve anything I set out to do—thank you.

To my daughter, who grew up thinking she needed me the most, when in reality, I truly needed her—thank you for saving my life.

And last, but certainly not least, to Charles Belcher—thank you for standing by my side as we fought the battle against the unknowns of living with NMOSD.

About the Author

Keisha Belcher became a professional, NC-licensed cosmetologist and makeup artist in 2000. In 2007, after being diagnosed with a rare neurological disorder called Neuromyelitis Optica, she shifted her focus to her health and her family.

In 2012, Keisha obtained her NC cosmetology instructor's license. The following year, in 2013, she decided to reinvent herself and launched her business, *Auxiliary Beauty Consultants*. Eager to take her business to the next level, she began researching, developing, and creating her company's own line of cosmetics, which includes signature lip glosses, lipsticks, and highly pigmented loose eyeshadows.

In 2014, Keisha was selected, along with several other talented makeup artists, to participate in Charlotte Fashion Week, where she provided makeup artistry for the runway models.

After many successful years in the cosmetology industry, Keisha chose to step outside of her comfort zone and earned her NC real estate license in 2021.

Currently, Keisha is working on a new project aimed at challenging stereotypical thinking and changing public perceptions. Through this initiative, she seeks to raise awareness about women with various disabilities who are courageously rising above their circumstances. By highlighting their beauty, strength, and accomplishments, Keisha hopes to inspire and empower others.

How to Connect with Keisha:

LinkedIn: Keisha Belcher
Facebook: @Keisha Belcher
Instagram: @keishabelcher1

The Force Behind the Storm
Kebra C. Moore, Visionary

Kebra C. Moore is a No. 1 Amazon bestselling author of four compelling novels, the founder and CEO of Welcome To The Storm

Publishing, and the visionary behind the powerful anthology series, Our Power – The Anthology. A passionate advocate, creator, and entrepreneur, Kebra uses every platform available to uplift and amplify the voices of women who are too often overlooked—especially those within the disability community.

A graduate of Claflin University, Kebra earned her degree in Music Education and has long blended her love for the arts with her commitment to advocacy. She is also an accomplished singer-songwriter; her original song *"He'll Make a Way"* was featured in the documentary *Becoming Barack*, chronicling the early life of President Barack Obama.

After surviving a life-altering spinal cord injury, Kebra made the decision to transform her pain into purpose. She realized that far too many stories from women with disabilities—particularly Black women—were being silenced or forgotten. Determined to change that, she launched *Our Power – The Anthology*, a collection built to showcase real, raw, and resilient voices from across the country.

The first volume, *Our Power – The Anthology: Melanated Queens Rising Beyond Disabilities*, was released in March 2025 and brought together powerful stories of survival and triumph from women who continue to defy the odds. It was followed by Volume II in July 2025, titled *Our Power – The Anthology: Four Women. Four Journeys. One Powerful Collection*, which highlighted the unique paths and shared strength of four extraordinary contributors. The series will continue with Volume III, *Our Power – The Anthology: Women in Leadership*, set for release in September 2025, centering the experiences of women who lead with grace, grit, and purpose despite the obstacles they face.

Outside of publishing, Kebra is the creator of the Tropical Storm Collection, a vibrant beauty line known for its bestselling matte lipsticks and the highly anticipated *Sunset Shades* eyeshadow palette. Her goal with every product is to help women feel bold, beautiful, and seen.

Kebra has been married for over 25 years and is the proud mother of two grown sons. She is also an active and financial member of Delta Sigma Theta Sorority, Incorporated, through which she continues to mentor, serve, and support communities in need.

In September 2025, Kebra will expand her mission even further by launching an 8-week course titled *"Start Your Own Publishing Company,"* where she will guide aspiring entrepreneurs through the fundamentals of building a fast-paced, sustainable publishing business—from forming an LLC and securing ISBNs, to formatting, distribution, marketing, and beyond.

Her journey is one of resilience, purpose, and undeniable power. Through every storm, she has found a way not just to survive—but to lead, create, and elevate others along the way.

To learn more about publishing your book or enrolling in Kebra's 8-week course, visit w2tspublishing.org.

www.ingramcontent.com/pod-product-compliance
Lightning Source LLC
Chambersburg PA
CBHW051228120626
46547CB00013B/1555